What Do We Know About the Roswell Incident?

by Ben

illustrated by Andrew Thomson

Penguin Workshop

For Bogo: IGNORE ALIEN ORDERS—BH

For Rhia and Cerys—AT

PENGUIN WORKSHOP
An imprint of Penguin Random House LLC, New York

First published in the United States of America by Penguin Workshop,
an imprint of Penguin Random House LLC, New York, 2023

Visit us online at penguinrandomhouse.com.

Library of Congress Control Number: 2022040636

Printed in the United States of America

ISBN 9780593519264 (paperback)   10 9 8 7 6 5 4 3 2   WOR
ISBN 9780593519271 (library binding)   10 9 8 7 6 5 4 3 2 1 WOR

Contents

What Do We Know About the Roswell Incident?

One hot July night in 1947, a strange thunderstorm struck the small town of Roswell, New Mexico. A local rancher saw lightning strike the same place repeatedly. Other residents reported a glowing object speeding across the sky. Some people heard thunderclaps, followed by an explosion. Was it possible that the explosion came from the nearby Roswell Army Air Field? Was this a storm, or something more frightening?

There was nothing reported about the night's events until a few days later. Then, the *Roswell Daily Record* newspaper printed an astonishing front page headline: "RAAF Captures Flying Saucer on Ranch in Roswell Region."

The twenty-five thousand residents of Roswell were shocked. The RAAF meant the Roswell Army Air Field. But what did they mean by *Flying Saucer*? Had the army found a spaceship? Were extraterrestrials—alien beings—now on Earth? And why had they chosen to land in Roswell? There were few details. The article said the flying saucer had crashed on a local ranch and was in army hands. Now, the residents of Roswell—and the world—wanted to know more.

Suddenly, everyone wanted to report on the story. The sheriff's office, military personnel at the RAAF, and the local newspapers and radio stations were swamped with calls from across America and beyond. National and international reporters were sent to Roswell to investigate. Overnight, the small town of Roswell seemed to become the center of the world's attention. But within twenty-four hours, everything changed.

The very next morning, the *Roswell Morning Dispatch* newspaper published a new front-page story: "Army Debunks Roswell Flying Disk as World Simmers with Excitement." This article said that the flying saucer had turned out to be the remains of a weather balloon. The balloon must have crashed to earth during the recent thunderstorm.

The weather balloon story made many people suspicious. It seemed like the army had accidently told the world about a crashed spaceship and now wanted to "cover it up." What then, had really happened during that stormy July night in Roswell? For over seventy years people have been trying to get to the bottom of this mystery. We know it today simply as "the Roswell Incident."

CHAPTER 1
Seeing UFOs

Roswell is no stranger to thunderstorms. The New Mexico city is a hot, dry place surrounded by dairy farms and dusty prairies. In summer, the daytime temperature often soars above 100°F.

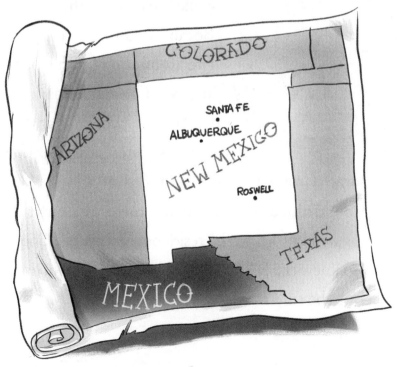

The heat can bring thunderstorms, tornadoes, and torrential rainfall. But aside from occasional extreme weather, Roswell in 1947 was a slow, sleepy place. Its main claim to fame was as the "Dairy Capital of the Southwest." But it was also home to one of the most secretive army airfields in the United States.

The RAAF was the headquarters of the 509th Bombardment Group—the world's only atomic strike force. It was the 509th Bomb Group that dropped two atomic bombs on Japan in 1945. This action marked the end of World War II. Two years later, the 509th Bomb Group was still stationed at the RAAF. Around three miles from the town, the airfield was well known to the residents of Roswell. They also knew the RAAF was a secretive place. No one could be sure what really went on there.

Nuclear weapons were not the only thing of interest to New Mexico's army bases in the 1940s. Unidentified flying objects (UFOs) were another. Today, we think of UFOs as spaceships from other planets. But in the 1940s, a UFO simply meant an unrecognized object in the sky. At that time, there were many reports from civilians who saw things they could not identify.

Top Secret New Mexico

During the 1940s, many top secret army experiments took place in New Mexico. The world's first nuclear weapons were developed there at the US army airfields in the towns of Los Alamos and Alamogordo. These weapons included the atomic and hydrogen bombs, which were powerful enough to destroy entire cities. The first atomic bomb was detonated in 1945 on the barren plains of the Alamogordo Bombing Range.

Some spy technology was also developed at New Mexico's airfields. Gathering information on the Soviet Union's nuclear development was of particular importance during the Cold War. If the Soviet Union developed its own nuclear bombs, it was feared they could be dropped on the United States.

Kenneth Arnold

One of the most famous early reports of a UFO sighting came from airplane pilot Kenneth Arnold. On June 24, 1947, Arnold was flying his small, one-engine plane near Mount Rainier in Washington State. Suddenly, several blue lights flashed in front of him. Then, nine triangular-shaped craft pulled up alongside his plane. The craft weaved from side to side and skimmed through the air "like a saucer if you skip it across the water." Arnold calculated that it took these nine craft one minute and forty-two seconds to fly the fifty miles between Mount Rainier and Mount Adams. This would mean their speed was about 1,700 miles per hour—three times faster than any aircraft of that time! Arnold said the objects did not seem to have pilots, and that the whole experience gave him "an eerie feeling."

Not everybody believed Arnold's account. Professional pilot E. J. Smith was skeptical. He said that he had never encountered a UFO, and what Arnold probably saw was "the reflection of his own instrument panel." But a few days later, Smith had an experience which changed his mind. E. J. Smith and his copilot Ralph Stevens were on a routine passenger flight between Idaho and Washington State when five disk-like objects appeared beside them. The pilots reported that

the disks flew in formation and then split off and
disappeared. Four more flying disks then appeared
and did the same thing. Could these have been the
same nine craft that Kenneth Arnold had seen?

After Smith's and Arnold's accounts, other people began saying they had also seen UFOs. Some said the UFOs looked like "long cigars," while others were "saucer" or "disk" shaped.

Afterward, the term "flying saucer" was often mentioned in newspaper articles about unidentified flying objects. Before long, saying "UFO" and "flying saucer" became common ways of describing what could be spaceships from other planets. Soon, lots of people in the United States began talking about UFOs. Many believed that extraterrestrials might be visiting Earth. The incident that took place in Roswell just a few weeks after the Arnold sighting greatly increased this belief.

CHAPTER 2
Crashed Wreckage

On July 2, 1947, the residents of Roswell, New Mexico, had no idea their town was about to become the UFO capital of America. Most residents were simply trying to stay cool on a particularly hot night. But nothing would prepare them for what came next. At around ten o'clock at night, Mary and Dan Wilmot were relaxing on their front porch. Suddenly, the couple saw a glowing object speeding across the sky. The

object looked "like two inverted saucers" and was around twenty feet wide. Dan estimated it was traveling between four hundred and five hundred miles per hour.

A few miles southwest of Roswell, James Woody and his son, William, had also seen something strange in the sky above their farm.

The object was large, bright, and had a long red light trail behind it. It moved fast and soon passed beyond their view. Woody assumed it was a meteorite crashing to earth.

On another farm outside Roswell, rancher William "Mac" Brazel watched with interest as a thunderstorm moved across the horizon.

But it was a strange storm. Lightning kept striking the same place over and over again. There were thunderclaps and then one loud explosion. Was this a storm, or a bomb, or a plane crash, he wondered? The next morning, he set out to investigate. A couple of miles from the ranch, Brazel found strange objects strewn across the land. There was silver metallic foil, lightweight wooden beams, and various pieces of plastic, rubber strips, and paper. The objects covered an area three quarters of a mile long by a few hundred feet wide. It looked like something had crashed and broken into pieces. Brazel collected a few of these pieces in his truck and drove back to the ranch.

Mac Brazel's neighbors were surprised by his find. Loretta and Floyd Proctor told Brazel about the recent reports of UFO sightings. They suggested he contact the local sheriff. The Proctors looked at the pieces Brazel had gathered.

Loretta Proctor said there was a wooden beam that looked like plastic or wood. Proctor said Brazel described other objects he had found. These included "metallic looking stuff that when you crushed it, it wouldn't stay crushed . . . and beams with pinkish-purple printing on it," Proctor said.

When Mac Brazel next drove into town on July 7, he brought the strange pieces of wreckage to show Sheriff George Wilcox. Wilcox thought the wreckage might have been connected with the army and called the airfield. The RAAF sent

Major Jesse Marcel

509th Bombardment Group intelligence officer Major Jesse Marcel to investigate.

Marcel and Brazel drove to the place where the pieces of wreckage had been found. Major Marcel bundled up as many pieces as he could into bags. On the way back to the RAAF, Marcel stopped by his house.

Although it was late at night, Marcel wanted to show the discovery to his wife, Viaud, and son, Jesse Jr. He brought the bags into the house

and emptied their contents onto the kitchen floor. He told Jesse Jr. that these may be parts of a flying saucer. Jesse Jr. later remembered the material consisting of a "thick, foil-like, metallic-gray substance" and wooden beams with "pink or purple" characters on them. The Marcels had not seen anything like them before.

Marcel delivered the bags of wreckage to the RAAF the next morning. From there, some of the bags were flown to Fort Worth Army Air Field in Texas, and on to Andrews Army Air Field in Washington, DC. Important, high-ranking officers were now taking an interest in what had been found at Roswell. Meanwhile, back at the RAAF, Commanding Officer Colonel William "Butch" Blanchard examined the wreckage. On July 8, a press release was sent to the local radio stations and newspapers. It said that a flying saucer had been discovered.

When the *Roswell Daily Record* newspaper published their article based on the press release, the town was stunned. There were hourly bulletins on the local radio stations KSWS and KGFL. The story quickly broke across the United States and then around the world. Everyone wanted details about the extraordinary news. *Roswell Morning Dispatch* Editor Arthur McQuiddy was swamped with calls. He said,

"I am a small editor in a small city in New Mexico talking to Paris, Rome, London, Tokyo . . . there was a lot of excitement."

But just as suddenly as the news broke, it was over. General Roger Ramey of the Fort Worth Army Air Field called a press conference. On the floor of his office, Ramey displayed what he said had been found at Roswell. The bits of foil, wood, and rubber belonged to a crashed

General Roger Ramey

weather balloon, Ramey explained. There had
been no flying saucer from another planet.

Newspapers across the world accepted what
Ramey said and published the updated weather
balloon story. There seemed little else for reporters
to investigate. As quickly as it had started, the
flying saucer story had died. But some Roswell
residents now found the US military behaving
strangely.

George "Jud" Roberts, co-owner of radio station KGFL, said he received a call from someone in a senator's office in Washington. Roberts was told that if KGFL put out any more stories about the incident, then the radio station would lose its broadcasting license.

There were greater threats. According to Sheriff George Wilcox's granddaughter, Barbara Dugger, Wilcox was visited by soldiers at his home. Dugger said that her grandmother told her that Wilcox was told he might be harmed if he talked about the incident.

Sheriff George Wilcox

Another of Mac Brazel's sons, Bill, said that his father was held for several days at the RAAF. He was questioned repeatedly about the find and sworn to secrecy. Bill said his father barely mentioned the incident afterward. However, the military had been too late to stop an interview Brazel had already given to reporters. In the interview, Brazel was clear about his discovery on the ranch. "I am sure what I found was not any weather observation balloon," Brazel said.

Men in Black

The legendary Men in Black (MIB) are thought
to be mysterious government agents whose job it
is to clean up, and cover up, evidence that alien
life forms have visited Earth. The goal of the MIB
is to erase any evidence that the United States
government is keeping its knowledge about
extraterrestrials secret.

The MIB are said to have visited people who claim to have witnessed UFO sightings and landings and told them to keep quiet about what they have seen. The MIB supposedly dress in plain, dark suits, which is where their nickname comes from.

In the early 1990s, author Lowell Cunningham and illustrator Sandy Carruthers created a comic book called *The Men in Black*, which was adapted into a feature film in 1997. The film, starring Will Smith and Tommy Lee Jones, was a box-office smash, and three sequels and an animated TV series followed.

CHAPTER 3
Cover-up

For more than thirty years, the Roswell Incident disappeared from view. Most people accepted the army's story about a crashed weather balloon. Those directly involved in the story kept silent about what they knew. But in the late 1970s, some of these people decided to speak out.

In 1978, now-retired intelligence officer Jesse Marcel gave an extraordinary interview. He said the army had lied about the Roswell Incident! Marcel told interviewers that the pieces of wreckage he had collected from Roswell were not the same as those displayed by General Ramey in his office. Ramey had substituted the Roswell pieces for bits of weather balloon.

This, Marcel now said, was because the army was covering up what it had really discovered.

Marcel said the actual pieces he had discovered were made from an unearthly material. It could not be burned, broken, or bent—even with a sledgehammer. "It was not anything from this Earth. That I'm quite sure of," Marcel said.

Marcel's interview instantly made the Roswell Incident a hot topic once again. UFOlogists (say: yoo-FOL-uh-jists)—investigators who believe extraterrestrials are visiting Earth—began to take an interest in Roswell. They looked for clues of an army cover-up. To do this, the investigators interviewed key people who had been present in 1947.

Some of these interviews were published in 1980 in an explosive book. *The Roswell Incident*, by Charles Berlitz and William Moore, featured interviews with Major Marcel and Colonel Thomas DuBose from Fort

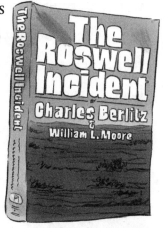

Worth Army Air Field. DuBose confirmed that General Ramey had ordered the original Roswell wreckage material be substituted for pieces of a weather balloon to show photographers.

DuBose later said that Ramey was acting under orders from Major General Clements McMullen, deputy commander of the Strategic Air Command at the Pentagon. The Pentagon is the headquarters of the US Department of Defense near Washington, DC, making McMullen one of the top military officers in the country. According to DuBose, McMullen said it was the "highest priority" to keep what had been discovered at Roswell secret. It was therefore up to Ramey to cover up the truth about what had been found.

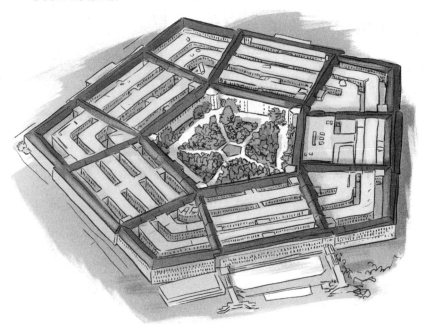

The Pentagon

The interviews with Marcel and DuBose seemed to prove what many people had long suspected—that there had been a cover-up at

Roswell. But what did the army have to hide? What had it really discovered crashed at Roswell?

The answer, according to *The Roswell Incident*, was a spaceship from another planet. The book said that in July 1947, this spaceship had likely been monitoring nuclear tests going on at New Mexico Air Fields. But then, the spaceship had been struck by lightning during a thunderstorm.

The lightning had knocked some pieces off the spaceship, but it flew a little farther before crashing. The pieces of the spaceship had later been found by rancher Mac Brazel. The spaceship itself lay some miles to the west. This meant there were actually two crash sites—one with pieces of wreckage and a second site with the spaceship.

Two people who had seen something crashing to Earth on July 2, 1947, were Roswell farmers James Woody and his son, William. They thought the object was a meteorite hitting the earth from space. The next day, the Woodys decided to locate the meteorite. They drove north for several miles on highway Route 285. But they discovered the road was blocked by military trucks and soldiers. They had to turn back.

The Woodys were the not the only ones to report a large military presence on Route 285. Paleontologist C. Bertrand Schultz and his colleagues had been digging for dinosaur fossils near the highway.

And there was an even more amazing eyewitness account described in *The Roswell Incident*. Civil engineer Grady "Barney" Barnett had been analyzing soil in the area when he saw a metallic object glinting in the distance. After driving toward the object, Barnett found a "disc-shaped object about twenty-five to thirty feet across." This was clearly a craft that had crashed and split apart. As he drew closer, Barnett saw bodies in the craft and on the ground outside it. Barnett said the bodies, dressed in gray jumpsuits, "were like humans but they were not humans. The heads were round, the eyes were small, and they had no hair . . . They were quite small by our standards and their heads were larger in proportion to their bodies than ours."

Barnett tried to get closer to the bodies, but military trucks began arriving. Soldiers cordoned off the area and an army officer spoke to Barnett.

The officer said Barnett had to leave and that he must never speak about what he had seen—to do so would be unpatriotic. For this reason, Barnett said, he had not talked about what he had seen for years afterward.

The eyewitness accounts published in *The Roswell Incident* made perfect sense to UFOlogists. They explained why the army had been so secretive about the 1947 events at Roswell. It was because the army had discovered

a flying saucer from another planet. After telling the press about the discovery, the army's top-ranking officers had panicked and changed their story. After all, they didn't yet know what they had found. Maybe the spaceship contained

a weapon that would give the United States absolute power in war? Or an exciting new technology? Whatever it was, the army decided that it had to remain top secret.

Grays

Grays, also known as "Gray Aliens" and "Roswell Grays," are claimed to be one type of extraterrestrial beings.

The first mention of Grays came from early science fiction books. But in 1961, New Hampshire couple Betty and Barney Hill reported that they were abducted by Grays and taken aboard a spaceship. They described their abductors as small and humanlike, with large, hairless heads, large black eyes, and gray skin. Grays have existed as a popular image of beings from another planet ever since.

CHAPTER 4
Extraterrestrial Bodies

The Roswell Incident was only one book written about the Roswell events of 1947. During the 1990s, several books were published about the alleged army cover-up. They provided eyewitness accounts as proof. Kevin Randle and Donald Schmitt's 1991 book *UFO Crash at Roswell* introduced an incredible account by Sergeant Frank Kaufmann.

Kaufmann said he was assigned to the RAAF in 1947 as part of a secret counterintelligence team (people who collect information to help prevent spying) code-named "Team Nine" or

"The Nine" because there were nine members. On the evening of July 2, 1947, Kaufmann was monitoring objects in the sky on the RAAF radar. (Radar uses radio waves to determine an object's location and speed.) For some hours Kaufmann watched a blip of light on the radar screen that moved very strangely. Then there was a flash and the blip disappeared.

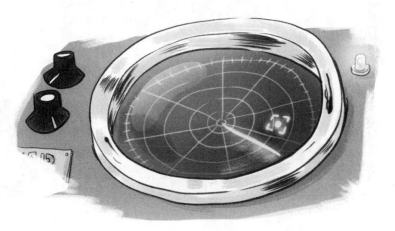

Assuming something had crashed, Kaufmann quickly gathered a group of soldiers to investigate. This team set out in a small convoy of trucks toward where the blip had last been seen. Just

before dawn, the convoy turned off Route
285 onto an unpaved road and then into open
country. Kaufmann was now following an eerie
light in the distance. When they neared the

light, the soldiers saw a crashed spaceship. The spaceship was about twenty-five feet long, round, with one triangular end. It had crashed into the bed of a dried-up creek.

Sergeant Frank Kaufmann

Sergeant Kaufmann said the bodies of two alien beings were lying next to the spaceship. They were a little more than five feet tall with large hairless heads and hands with five fingers. They were wearing silver jumpsuits. He said the alien beings were clearly dead, and their bodies were starting to deteriorate in the heat. The bodies were put into lead-lined body bags and transported quickly to the RAAF hospital.

Another soldier also supported the existence of this crash site. Military photographer Sergeant Frederick Benthal said he was picked up from the RAAF by a military truck one morning. While driving to an unknown destination, Benthal was told to put on a full-body rubberized suit for "protection." After the truck turned off the highway, Benthal saw activity everywhere.

Several tents had been set up and large, bright lights were everywhere. Soldiers were loading unrecognizable objects aboard military trucks. When his truck parked, Benthal was ordered into a tent. Here, several dead bodies lay underneath

a tarp on the ground. The tarp was pulled back so Benthal could photograph the bodies. He immediately realized they were not human. They were all small, thin, and had large heads. After taking photos, Benthal had his camera equipment confiscated and was sworn to lifelong

secrecy. Benthal said he was then reassigned to Antarctica—the southernmost region on Earth—to make sure he was out of the way.

So what happened to these bodies? In *The Truth About the UFO Crash at Roswell*, another eyewitness offered an explanation. In 1947, W. Glenn Dennis was a mortician working at Roswell's Ballard Funeral Home. Dennis supplied coffins to the RAAF and provided ambulances for wounded airmen. Early in the afternoon of July 5, Dennis received a call from the RAAF asking how

Glenn Dennis

to preserve bodies that had "been laying out in the elements." He was also asked if he had any child-size coffins. Dennis assumed there had been a plane crash, but heard nothing more about it.

Later that afternoon, Dennis was asked to take an injured airman to the RAAF hospital. As he helped the airman into the hospital back door, Dennis noticed several military field ambulances nearby. One had its door open, and Dennis could see a type of "metal canoe" inside. This was a bluish color and looked like it had been exposed to high temperatures. Along the side was strange writing or symbols Dennis said looked "like Egyptian hieroglyphics."

Inside the hospital, Dennis saw a nurse that he knew running from an examining room. The nurse, named Naomi Self, had a towel over her face and seemed upset. When Self saw Dennis, she cried, "My gosh, get out of here or you're going to be in a lot of trouble." She then ran into another room. Dennis found an officer and told him that he was available to help if there had been a plane crash in the desert. But before he knew it, Dennis found himself being escorted

from the hospital by two military policemen. At the back door, Dennis was stopped by another army officer with the "meanest-looking eyes I ever saw." The officer told Dennis sternly, "You did not see anything, there was no crash here, and if you say anything you could get into a lot of trouble." Shaken up, Dennis left the hospital.

The next morning, Dennis received a call from Naomi Self. She wanted to meet. Over lunch, Self told Dennis that she had been helping with an autopsy on three extraterrestrial bodies.

An autopsy is a medical procedure to establish a cause of death. Self said the bodies were three to four feet tall with large heads. They had two small holes for a nose and a slit for a mouth. She said they were badly damaged and gave off a terrible odor. The smell was so bad that Self had run from the examining room to be sick. It was at this point she saw Dennis.

The lunchtime meeting was the last time Dennis saw Naomi Self. He tried to contact her afterward, but was told she had been transferred out of the country. This seemed strange. Would the US government really go that far to keep its secret?

By the mid-1990s, conspiracy theories about the supposed Roswell cover-up were everywhere. A conspiracy theory is a belief that a powerful organization is responsible for a particular event, but is keeping it secret, or covering it up. Books, articles, documentaries, and television shows seemed to agree that the army had found a spaceship with extraterrestrials at Roswell. Glenn Dennis even helped found a UFO museum in Roswell.

If all this was true, then where were the extraterrestrial bodies and spaceship now? And which branch of government was hiding them?

Many UFOlogists believed that agencies such as the Central Intelligence Agency (CIA) and the Federal Bureau of Investigation (FBI) would have to have been involved. Frank Kaufmann said the cover-up went to the top levels of government, and even "to the president."

Area 51

Area 51 is a US Air Force base located at Groom Lake, Nevada. Covering more than four hundred square miles of desert, Area 51 was originally used by the CIA to test experimental weapons and aircraft. Only people with high-level security clearance can enter. But in 1989, a former Area 51 security guard named Bob Lazar broke his oath of secrecy to talk about the military base. Lazar said that spacecraft and extraterrestrial bodies were being stored in a hangar there. This convinced many people that the evidence from the Roswell incident was being kept at Area 51.

CHAPTER 5
The Roswell Report

In the 1990s, the Roswell Incident was a story that refused to go away. The US Air Force continued to deny the existence of a spacecraft or alien beings. But there was growing pressure from the public for the air force to release any information it had. A US representative for New Mexico, Congressman Steven Schiff, even got involved.

Steven Schiff

Schiff said he had received a number of inquiries about the Roswell Incident from UFOlogists, Roswell residents, and even soldiers who had served at the RAAF in 1947. He said it was time the air force told the truth about what had taken place at Roswell more than forty years earlier.

In 1993, Congressman Schiff asked the air force to declassify (make public) all its material on the Roswell Incident. The air force said the information it had was in the US National Archives. This included Project Blue Book, which contains the air force's own investigations into UFOs.

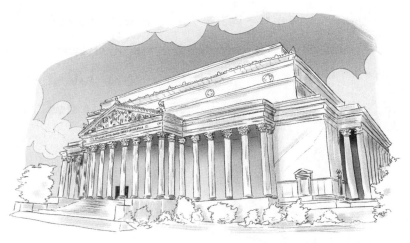

National Archives Building

Project Blue Book

Project Blue Book was the US Air Force's report of its investigations into UFO sightings reported between 1947 and 1969. The purpose of these investigations was to follow up on citizens' reports of UFOs and to find explanations. The investigation also aimed to determine if any of the UFOs could be a threat to national security.

Project Blue Book investigated 12,618 UFO sightings over the years, 701 of which remained "Unidentified." It was decided the others were  human aircraft or natural phenomena, such as stars or clouds.

The Roswell Incident does not appear in Project Blue Book reports.

The National Archives did not have any details about Roswell, and so Schiff asked the General Accounting Office (GAO) to get involved. The GAO is one of the most powerful investigating bodies in America. As soon as it began looking into the Roswell Incident, the air force suddenly produced its own report on the matter.

The report was called *The Roswell Report: Fact versus Fiction in the New Mexico Desert.* Surprisingly, it admitted that the original weather balloon story had been a lie. It confirmed that the story had been made up to hide the truth about what had crashed at Roswell. However, it had not been a UFO that had crashed. Instead, the air force said it had been a damaged balloon that was part of Project Mogul—a top secret surveillance program to spy on the Soviet Union.

Project Mogul used high-altitude balloons with microphones that could detect sound waves created by an atomic bomb blast. This would show whether the Soviet Union had developed nuclear weapons. The air force report said a crashed Project Mogul balloon was the source of the wreckage at Roswell. The balloons used in Project Mogul were enormous. They were made up of more than twenty balloons—some fifteen feet wide or larger—on a long line of nylon wire. The line measured more than six hundred feet long and hung like a kite tail in the sky with silver-foil radar reflectors attached so the balloon could be tracked. Microphones shaped like tubes hung from the bottom of the nylon wire.

The balloons themselves were made from neoprene and polyethylene—types of lightweight plastic—and coated in aluminium. This material, the report said, was consistent with the discovery at Roswell of "metal-like materials that when wadded into a ball, return to their original shape."

The other materials used for the balloons included wooden beams, foil, parchment-type paper, and reinforcing tape. This tape came from a toy company and was covered in pink and purple "symbols such as arcs, flowers, circles and diamonds," the report said. The report also said a crashed balloon would have scattered its pieces over a large area.

Several Project Mogul balloons had been released from New Mexico's Alamogordo Army Air Field that were not recovered. One of these balloons had been released on June 4. This, the report concluded, probably made up the wreckage found by Mac Brazel.

The report made a lot of sense. Project Mogul was a top secret program that was highly classified—meaning not many people knew about it. Was it possible that those working on Project Mogul saw the original flying saucer newspaper story and panicked? They would have

known it was not a flying saucer, but instead their missing Project Mogul balloon. To keep the project secret, the Project Mogul team probably called Major General McMullen, who then ordered the cover-up. General Ramey invented the weather balloon story as a result.

Project Mogul therefore seemed like a logical explanation that tied up many loose ends. The toy company tape with pink and purple symbols certainly explained eyewitness accounts of "strange hieroglyphs." But did the public accept the air force report?

One person who remained skeptical was Congressman Steven Schiff: "We've had three explanations from the military about what crashed: the first explanation is a flying saucer, they changed that and said we made a mistake, it's a weather balloon . . . and now we have a third explanation."

Was Project Mogul therefore just another part of the air force's ongoing cover-up? Was the US government still trying to hide a crashed spaceship and extraterrestrial bodies? What about the eyewitnesses who swore to seeing these things?

One problem with eyewitnesses is that they can be unreliable—especially nearly fifty years after an event. It is common for people to remember things incorrectly. Eyewitness accounts do not by themselves provide solid proof. And what investigators into the Roswell Incident wanted was actual evidence that extraterrestrials had crashed on Earth. This evidence could be an alien being's body, part of a spaceship, or photographs, or even a film showing these things.

Then, incredibly, the evidence seemed to appear in 1995.

CHAPTER 6
The Alien Autopsy Film

Reg Presley

In 1995, British pop star Reg Presley made an astonishing announcement. Presley said he had seen a film of the autopsy of an alien being from Roswell. Soon afterward, a music producer named

Ray Santilli said he had the world's only copy of the film. Santilli said the film had been purchased from an elderly military cameraman. The cameraman had been in the US army in 1947 and was asked to film the medical examination.

Ray Santilli

On May 5, 1995, Santilli showed the black-and-white film to journalists, UFOlogists, and television producers at the Museum of London. The images astounded the audience.

The film shows a lifeless body on a table in the middle of an operating theater. It has a round belly, a hairless head, and large black eyes. There are six fingers on the being's hands, and its

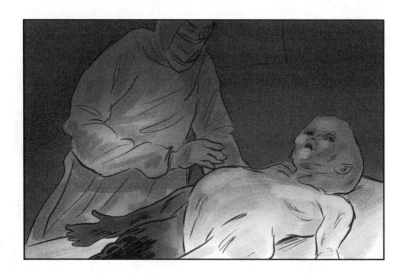

left leg appears black and decomposed. Doctors dressed head to toe in white protective clothing circle the body performing the autopsy. Nearby, there are tables with assorted pieces of metal showing strange lettering and hand symbols.

The seventeen-minute-long film caused a great sensation. It became known as the "alien autopsy film." Many accepted that the film was the proof about the Roswell incident they had always wanted. Others questioned whether the film was real, or a hoax. A hoax is something that has been created to look real to fool people, like a complex prank.

Journalists wanted to know more about where the film had come from. Who was the cameraman? Could they interview him? Santilli said the cameraman wanted to remain anonymous, but that the film was indeed real. It had been taken at Alamogordo Army Air Field.

After the film was shown in London, an American television documentary promised to uncover the truth about whether or not it was real. The documentary *Alien Autopsy: Fact or Fiction?* was broadcast on the Fox television network on August 28, 1995. It was so popular that it was shown two more times.

ALIEN AUTOPSY: (fact or fiction?)

IN 1947, SOMETHING HAPPENED IN ROSWELL, NEW MEXICO...

The documentary crew interviewed film industry professionals, such as a special effects expert. Most of these people said the film looked real. Also interviewed was famous forensic pathologist (a doctor who carries out autopsies) Cyril Wecht. Wecht said the autopsy procedures in the film looked genuine.

Cyril Wecht

What did the eyewitnesses to the Roswell Incident think? A British Broadcasting Company

(BBC) journalist showed them the film to find out. Jesse Marcel Jr.'s father had shown him Roswell wreckage in 1947. Jesse Jr. said the writing on the metal from the alien autopsy film looked "vaguely similar to what I saw." He was not sure if the film was a hoax. Neither was Frank Kaufmann, who claimed to have seen the actual extraterrestrials. Kaufmann said the bodies he saw did not have six fingers, unlike those shown in the alien autopsy film. "It doesn't look too close to the Roswell Incident," Kaufmann added.

Even though the documentary did not prove that the film was real, it fascinated people for many years to come.

The X-Files

In the 1990s, there were several movies and TV shows about government cover-ups and conspiracies. *The X-Files* was one of the longest running and most popular science fiction series on television. It's tagline (a phrase used as a sort of slogan) was "The Truth Is Out There."

In the show, FBI Special Agents Fox Mulder and Dana Scully investigate strange and unexplained cases, known as "X-Files." Mulder is desperate to uncover evidence of extraterrestrials on Earth. Scully, a doctor, is skeptical about their existence. They eventually discover the government is keeping the existence of extraterrestrials secret.

On *The X-Files*, Special Agent Fox Mulder was played by actor David Duchovny and Special Agent Dana Scully was played by actor Gillian Anderson.

The real FBI does have a file on UFO sightings and the Roswell Incident. These files were declassified in 2011 and can be viewed in the FBI's online "Vault." However, there is nothing in them to suggest evidence of either UFOs or extraterrestrials.

CHAPTER 7
Case Closed?

The alien autopsy film showed that many people still believed in the existence of Roswell extraterrestrials, even after nearly fifty years. In 1997, on the fiftieth anniversary of the Roswell Incident, a CNN/*TIME* poll found that almost two-thirds of Americans surveyed believed a spaceship had crashed at Roswell. Eighty percent said the government was hiding information about alien beings. Many people criticized the air force's 1995 report. They said it did not once mention eyewitness accounts of extraterrestrials. Did this mean the existence of bodies was still being covered up?

In response, the US Air Force released another report in 1997. *The Roswell Report: Case Closed* aimed to answer any remaining questions about extraterrestrials at Roswell. It did this by giving details of New Mexico Air Force programs from the 1940s and 1950s.

There were two programs, High Dive and Excelsior, that tested parachutes at high altitudes. This was because jets were being developed to fly higher than before. If the pilots ejected, they would need to parachute to earth safely. To test this, parachutes with crash test dummies were dropped out of balloons at altitudes of up to ninety-eight thousand feet. Crash test dummies are plastic, human-shaped models used to test the impact of car crashes.

When the High Dive and Excelsior crash test dummies landed, military trucks raced to collect them. *The Roswell Report: Case Closed* said these truck convoys were similar to the crash-site scenes described by eyewitnesses in 1947. *Case Closed* said the crash test dummies could have been mistaken for extraterrestrials. They were hairless and some wore gray jumpsuits, just like the descriptions of extraterrestrials. They were also strapped to gurneys (wheeled stretchers), making them look deceased.

Crash test dummy

The Roswell Report: Case Closed also addressed mortician Glenn Dennis's claims about an autopsy at the Roswell Army Air Field hospital. The report said Dennis may have been referring to an accident at the RAAF. The air force said a KC-97G supply plane had exploded on the runway and eleven airmen died. Their bodies were terribly burned and disfigured. They were taken to the RAAF hospital for autopsies. The doctors said the smell of these burned bodies was overpowering. The report said nurse Naomi Self may have mistaken these bodies for extraterrestrials.

The report concluded that there was no evidence of extraterrestrials found in the area. It said that other Roswell eyewitnesses confused their accounts with real events. Some had lied deliberately. These people were "attempting to perpetrate a hoax, believing that no serious effort would ever be taken to verify their stories," the report said.

Many people criticized the report. They said the runway accident had happened in 1956, nearly ten years *after* the Roswell Incident! The Project High Dive and Project Excelsior programs ran between 1947 and 1959, and mostly took place in the 1950s. And the crash test dummies were six feet tall, not four to five feet tall as eyewitnesses had described the extraterrestrials.

Once again UFOlogists and others investigating the Roswell Incident were unconvinced. The 1997 report seemed like

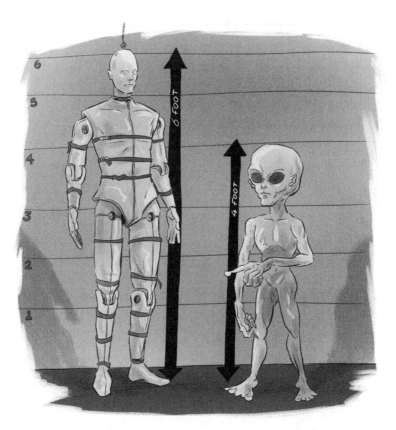

another desperate government attempt to cover up what had happened. So what was the truth? Would the stories about Roswell extraterrestrials and crashed spaceships ever go away?

CHAPTER 8
The Truth Is Out There

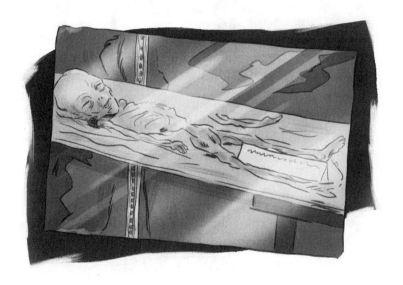

In 2014, the Roswell Incident was once again making news. Two photographic slides had been found among the property of a recently deceased Arizona woman. The slides showed a small, humanlike body with a large head. The body was lying in a glass case with a sign that was too blurry to read. The slide was shown to Thomas Carey and Donald Schmitt, authors of the 2007 book *Witness to Roswell*. Like many Roswell authors, Carey and Schmitt had spent years trying to prove that extraterrestrials had crash-landed in Roswell. Could these slides provide this proof?

After investigating, Carey and Schmitt concluded the slides were indeed images of an extraterrestrial body. At a 2014 UFO conference at American University, in Washington, DC, Carey told the world, "We have the smoking

Thomas Carey   Donald Schmitt

gun!" This meant they had actual evidence of extraterrestrials. They promised to show the world this evidence at their own conference in Mexico City, Mexico, in 2015. Nearly seven thousand people paid between $20 and $86 to attend this conference, called BeWitness. UFOlogists, authors, and other experts spoke at the conference before the slides were shown on a big screen.

Three days later, there was another bombshell. Somebody had used an online software program to unblur the placard on the slide. It read: "Mummified Body of a Two Year Old Boy." The slide's image was not of an alien being, but an exhibit from a Colorado museum.

Comments about the discovery were immediately posted online. "The Smoking Gun: RIP (rest in peace) To the Roswell Slides" said one. "Fraud Put To Rest" said another. Carey and Schmitt said they didn't mean to deceive anyone. They thought the slides were genuine. But sadly, in the hunt for proof of Roswell extraterrestrials, people have lied before.

In the 2000s, many Roswell theories and eyewitness accounts were proven to be false. In 2006, the man who had shown the alien autopsy film to the world admitted it was a not real. Ray Santilli said the fake autopsy had been staged and filmed in an apartment in London. The extraterrestrial body had been made from foam and latex by a sculptor named John Humphreys.

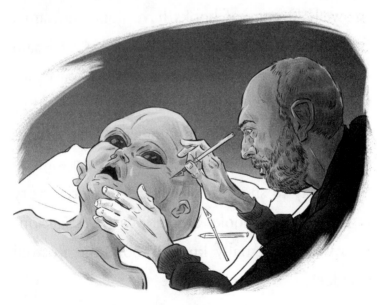

The inside of the body was filled with animal parts, including sheep brains. Humphreys and his friends then dressed up like doctors while another recorded "the autopsy" on an old handheld camera.

Santilli, it appears, had made the film to trick people and to make money. Over time, the Roswell Incident itself has become a moneymaking industry. Many documentaries and television shows have investigated the 1947 events at Roswell. Dozens of books have done the same. Some sensational books make big claims. One said that material recovered from a crashed spacecraft had been given to private US companies so they could develop new technologies. Other books were written by hopeful UFOlogists who want to find a way to show that the extraterrestrial story is true. A few books are serious investigations into what is actually known about the Roswell Incident.

Former CIA officer Karl Pflock set out to do just that in his 2001 book, *Roswell: Inconvenient Facts and the Will to Believe*. Pflock found the accounts of several eyewitnesses to be unreliable. One of these eyewitnesses was Glenn Dennis, who said that nurse Naomi Self had told him about an alien autopsy. But Pflock discovered that no one of that name ever worked at the RAAF! Naomi Self did not seem to exist. Pflock also found

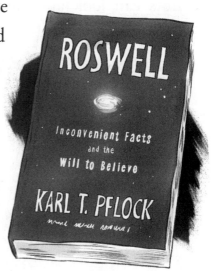

that accounts by eyewitness Frank Kaufmann had changed and become more fantastic over time. Did Kaufmann really see a crashed extraterrestrial spacecraft, or did he just get carried away with his own story?

To date, eyewitness accounts provide the only detailed stories of Roswell extraterrestrials. And yet, Roswell itself is a city dedicated to the Roswell Incident. Attractions include the International UFO Museum and Research Center, where visitors can look at exhibits about the Roswell

Incident and have their photos taken with models of alien beings. There is also the Roswell UFO Spacewalk, a flying saucer–shaped McDonald's, and streetlights shaped like the heads of Grays.

It's fun to visit these sites, but many people also hope that some part of the Roswell story is true.

Is it possible aliens have indeed visited Earth—if not at Roswell, then elsewhere? Who would know the truth about this? The president of the United States receives classified information about UFO sightings when they take office. So what have former presidents said about Roswell?

Former US president Bill Clinton said he had checked the records about Roswell extraterrestrials before the fiftieth anniversary of the Roswell Incident. He said, "When the Roswell thing came up, I knew we'd get gazillions of letters, so I had the Roswell papers reviewed." But he confirmed there were no aliens there. However, Clinton did say the existence of aliens on other planets is likely: "We know there are billions of stars and planets, literally out there . . . if we were visited someday, I wouldn't be surprised."

Bill Clinton

Former US president Barack Obama also said there was little top secret information about the Roswell Incident. Declassified FBI and CIA files from the late 1970s onward say the same. However in 2021, Obama admitted there had been some UFO sightings that nobody could explain: "There's footage and records of objects in the skies that we don't know exactly what they are, we can't explain how they moved, their trajectory. They did not have an easily explainable pattern."

Barack Obama

Incredibly, some of this footage was revealed by the US Navy in 2021. The navy said it had an active program that studied unusual encounters between military pilots and UFOs. The Unidentified Aerial Phenomenon (UAP) Task Force has footage of unexplained flying objects shaped like spheres and acorns. They are shown flying faster than any known craft on Earth.

On June 25, 2021, a report on these objects was published by the US Office of the Director of National Intelligence. The report looked at 144 observations of unidentified objects seen by navy pilots between 2004 and 2021. Its findings, however, were "largely inconclusive." It said one of the objects was simply a large, deflating balloon. It did not know what the other 143 were.

Interestingly, not all of the report was made public. Some of it remains classified. Does this mean the US government is hiding something it doesn't want the public to know about? Is there another UFO cover-up going on? Some people in Roswell, New Mexico, continue to believe that the truth about UFOs remains hidden. Is it possible that part of an alien ship is still buried in the dry, desert ground outside their small town? Many believe the truth *is* out there.

Timeline of the Roswell Incident

1947 — The *Roswell Daily Record* reports the army has found a crashed flying saucer; the next day, the *Roswell Dispatch* reports the flying saucer was a weather balloon

1978 — Former intelligence officer Jesse Marcel says the army lied about the weather balloon to cover up what was found at Roswell

1989 — Former area 51 security guard Bob Lazar says extraterrestrial bodies were being stored at US Air Force facility Area 51 in the Nevada desert

1993 — Congressman Steven Schiff calls on the air force to release its classified files into the Roswell incident

1994 — The US Air Force releases *The Roswell Report: Fact versus Fiction in the New Mexico Desert*, which it says explains the events in Roswell in 1947

1997 — The US Air Force releases *The Roswell Report: Case Closed*, another report it says will clear up the events at Roswell in 1947

2014 — Former president Bill Clinton says no extraterrestrials were discovered at Roswell

2021 — The US Navy produces a report into "Unidentified Aerial Phenomenon," a new name for UFOs; its findings are inconclusive

Timeline of the World

1947 — The US Central Intelligence Agency (CIA) is formed, tasked with gathering national security information

1950 — The Korean War between North and South Korea begins. The United States supports South Korea, and China and the Soviet Union support North Korea

1961 — John F. Kennedy becomes the thirty-fifth president of the United States

1963 — Martin Luther King Jr. organizes the March on Washington for Jobs and Freedom

1969 — US astronaut Neil Armstrong becomes the first person to walk on the moon

1977 — Director George Lucas's new movie *Star Wars* hits theaters; it is later renamed *Star Wars IV: A New Hope*

1986 — An accident at the Chernobyl Nuclear Power Plant causes a nuclear meltdown in the Ukraine city of Pripyat

1998 — The search engine Google is founded by Stanford University students Larry Page and Sergey Brin

2011 — The world population reaches seven billion people

2020 — The vaccination program begins for COVID-19, a disease that started a global pandemic

2021 — President Joe Biden orders the withdrawal of US troops and personnel from Afghanistan after twenty years of military operations

Bibliography

*Books for young readers

Berliner, Don, and Stanton T. Friedman. *Crash at Corona: The US Military Retrieval and Cover-Up of a UFO*. New York: Paraview Special Editions, 2004.

Berlitz, Charles, and William L. Moore. *The Roswell Incident*. New York: Grosset & Dunlap, 1980.

Carey, Thomas J., and Donald R. Schmitt. *The Roswell Incident: An Eyewitness Account*. New York: Rosen Publishing Group, 2012.

Carey, Thomas J., and Donald R. Schmitt. *Witness to Roswell*. Franklin Lakes, NJ: The Career Press, 2007.

*DeMolay, Jack. *UFOs: The Roswell Incident*. New York: Rosen Publishing Group, 2007.

*Hoena, Blake. *The Roswell UFO Incident*. Minnetonka, MN: Black Sheep, 2020.

*Manzanero, Paula K. *Where Is Area 51?* New York:
     Penguin Workshop, 2018.

Marrs, Jim. *Alien Agenda*. New York: HarperCollins, 1997.

Pflock, Karl T. *Roswell: Inconvenient Facts and the Will to
     Believe*. Amherst, NY: Prometheus Books, 2001.

Randle, Kevin D., and Donald R. Schmitt. *UFO Crash at Roswell*.
     New York: Avon Books, 1991.

Saler, Benson, Charles A. Ziegler, and Charles B. Moore. *UFO Crash
     at Roswell: The Genesis of a Modern Myth*. Old Saybrook, CT:
     Konecky & Konecky, 1997.

US Air Force. *The Roswell Report: Case Closed*. Washington, DC:
     US Government Printing Office, 1997.

US Air Force. *The Roswell Report: Fact versus Fiction in the New
     Mexico Desert*. Washington, DC: US Government Printing
     Office, 1995.